God [...] Than ANY Sword

A Survivor's Story

THE BELIZE TIMES

50 cts

SUNDAY MAY 7, 1989

Masked Man Terrorizes Church Service

BELIZE CITY, TIMES, May 6
A religious crusade held by the Tabernacle of Praise Church last night on the football field behind the Princess Royal Youth Hostel, turned into bloody horror and mad confusion when a reputed marksman wielding a machete began chopping people at random.

People, screaming in terror, were seen running in all directions as they attempted to get away from the sweeping blade of the machete.

When it was over some persons were injured, two of them seriously. The Crusade, into its second night, had lost before the incident occurred.

Mrs. Ruperta Narien, a U.S. citizen from New York, received

later fell off, would have done more damage since it cut to the bone.

Mr. Albert DeSouza.

When the machete man attacked Mr. De Souza, who was on the platform, Mr. De Souza hit him in the chest with a microphone stand and the machete man ran off.

Miss Sandra Malder, the 15 year old daughter of Miss Genevieve Malder, one of the injured told AMATRAULA she witnessed the incident from her verandah.

"I was standing on my verandah when all of a sudden I heard screaming and saw people running in all directions," said Miss Elizabeth Malder and her brother, Mr. Gustavo, who did not want his to go near the field because of

later fell off, would have done more damage since it cut to the bone.

Mr. Albert DeSouza.

When the machete man attacked Mr. De Souza, who was on the platform, Mr. De Souza hit him in the chest with a microphone stand and the machete man ran off.

Miss Sandra Malder, the 15 year old daughter of Miss Genevieve Malder, one of the injured told AMATRAULA she witnessed the incident from her verandah.

"I was standing on my verandah when all of a sudden I heard screaming and saw people running in all directions," said Miss Malder.

Miss Malder, who did not read his

by

Evangelist Yvonne Ruperta Narain

God Is Greater Than Any Sword
Copyright © 2000 by Yvonne Narain
ALL RIGHTS RESERVED

All Scripture references are from the Authorized King James Version of the Bible.

Fairmont Books is a ministry of The McDougal Foundation, Inc., a Maryland nonprofit corporation dedicated to spreading the Gospel of the Lord Jesus Christ to as many people as possible in the shortest time possible.

Fairmont Books
P.O. Box 3595
Hagerstown, MD 21742-3595
www.mcdougalpublishing.com

ISBN 1-58158-017-7

Printed in the United States of America
For Worldwide Distribution

Dedication

This book is dedicated to my husband, Aubron E. Narain, who always supports me in doing God's work. I would not have made it this far without his support.

To our three sons, Edwin, Marty and Garin Narain, whose strength, prayers and love helped me to make it through the time of my recovery and are still supporting me today. I love you!

Acknowledgments

I would like to acknowledge the following special people in my life:

My mother, Mrs. Grace Price, for the godly upbringing she gave me and for her strength and love.

My sisters and brothers, let us continue to keep the bond of unity and love.

My father, Mr. Egbert Price, who has gone on to be with the Lord, for the knowledge, wisdom and faith that he imparted to me, something that money cannot buy. I miss you.

Rev. Stanley Kidd, pastor of Bethlehem Missionary Church, for preaching the uncompromised Word of God that helped me to live a more godly life.

My sister-in law, Schefflin Narain, who stood with me in my trial and who supports me spiritually and physically.

Contents

Tribute From Aubron Narain 6
Foreword by Dorothy Allen 7
Introduction 9

1. A Childhood Desire 11
2. Farewell, Lovely Isle 14
3. My First Missionary Endeavors 20
4. Chaos in Belize City 26
5. Miracle Upon Miracle 34
6. God's Protection 42
7. Complete Restoration 47
8. God Was Glorified 51
9. A Very Important Dream 56
10. A World in Need of Love 62
11. By His Stripes 67
12. Don't Wait Until I'm Gone 71

Epilogue 75

About the Author 77

Tract Ordering Information 80

Tribute

My wife, author Yvonne Ruperta Narain, has shown me by example what it means to be faithful, dedicated, obedient and committed to God and to our family in both good and bad times. Thank you for your love and sacrifice. I love you.

Aubron Narain

Foreword

More than fourteen years ago I became acquainted with Evangelist Yvonne R. Narain as we were members of the same church in Queens, New York. We later relocated to Florida. Evangelist Narain's main focus is to fulfill God's will for her life, lead lost souls to Christ and live pleasing to Him. As an ordained minister and evangelist, she preaches in various churches, blessing many hearts and seeing lives being saved by the power of God.

As wife and mother, Sister Narain is exemplary. As a missionary, she is extraordinary. Though working a full-time job, she still finds time to travel to the West Indies and South America, proclaiming the Good News of salvation and ministering to the spiritual and physical needs of adults and children. She is a source of encouragement to me, her church, her community and to all who know her. She is always ready to encourage others in the Lord.

Jesus commanded us in Matthew 28:19 to *"teach all nations."* With the determination to be obedient to God's will, this young woman has encountered dramatic and traumatic experiences, some of which are told in this book. Readers will see how the mighty hand of God brought her through every situation.

Books can transform lives and ministries. May this one be an inspiration and encouragement to all who read it. My prayer is that some mission-minded person or persons, through the anointing of the Holy Spirit, will pick up the mantle like Elisha did and run with it.

As you read this book, allow the love of God to touch your heart, and He will use you for His glory in whatever way He sees fit.

Sister Dorothy Allen

Introduction

This book is based on a true story and is intended to encourage believers everywhere to trust God fully, even when they are going through trials and problems in their lives. Always remember that there is nothing too hard for God to do. The trials will come, but God will be with you, and will see you through them — if you trust Him. Do not get discouraged and give up. This is what the enemy wants. Call on the name of the Lord; He has given us that authority.

Give of yourself to His service. Live life so that others will see Jesus in and through you. Our God is great and He can deliver us from anything that tries to hinder our Christian experience.

The book is also intended to let nonbelievers know that God is real and that He is coming back to Earth one day soon to receive those who have prepared themselves to live with Him. He is a God of love and compassion, and He is waiting patiently for you to accept Him as Lord of your life.

Yvonne Ruperta Narain
Plantation, Florida

In my distress I cried unto the Lord, *and he heard me.* Psalm 120:1

Chapter One

A Childhood Desire

When I was still a very small girl living in my native Honduras, somehow I already knew that I wanted to be a missionary.

Life on the Bay Islands, where I grew up, was simple, calm and peaceful. The lifestyle was one of serenity. My island is called Roatan. Everyone on the island knew each other. If we went to a store, to the movies or to church, we saw the same people. All the people on the island were one big happy family, and everyone loved the Lord.

People on our island were very respectful of each other and cared for one another. When some of the islanders were sick or hurt, some of us younger ones were sent to their homes to help them. I always enjoyed these assignments.

Helping others brought such great joy to my heart that I told my Sunday school teachers, my friends and my family very early in life that when I grew up I would be a missionary so that I could help more people. I would go all over the world witnessing for Christ and helping people in any way I could.

I had met missionaries who came to the island to have revival, as well as Peace Corps workers who came to help our people with medical issues. Some Christians came to help us build churches or houses for our people or whatever else was needed. I thought they were wonderful, and I wanted to do what they did someday.

Our people deeply appreciated these visits and worked well with the visitors, so that they kept coming back. "The people here are very kind and polite," they told us. The next time they came, they would bring others with them. Ours was indeed a good life.

Crime was nearly nonexistent where we lived. In the entire time I lived there, I heard of only one killing, and it was love related. A girl was threatening to leave her boyfriend, so he took both of their lives. That incident was talked about for many months because we had so little else of a sordid nature to interest us.

How I loved the Bay Island of Roatan! It was full of tropical fruit trees and lovely white sand beaches along the two-tone blue seashore. The temperature rarely dipped below seventy or rose above ninety degrees. On the coldest days, the range would be somewhere in the sixties. That was our "winter" (December and January).

Around the island, we had an abundance of seafood: lobsters, crabs, conchs, shrimp and fish. We ate these seafoods nearly every day, and many of our islanders lived by fishing.

Our pastimes were baseball, fishing and swimming. What a life!

My desire to be a missionary and, particularly, a soul-winner, was fortified in 1977 when one of my brothers was killed at the young age of twenty-six. He had not been serving the Lord, and it was uncertain if he had had time to ask God for forgiveness before he died. I was shaken by this experience and decided to dedicate my life to encouraging people everywhere to accept the Lord while they had time and not to wait for the last minute. Who knows if we will even have a last minute?

Death was no respecter of persons. It came to young and old alike. It came to men and women alike. Even boys and girls sometimes died, and even babies. Death is universal. I had to help people be prepared for whenever and however death came, for the Scriptures taught:

> *It is appointed unto men once to die, but after this the judgment.*   Hebrews 9:27

Chapter Two

Farewell, Lovely Isle

As much as I loved the Bay Islands, I began to realize as a teenager that my life would go nowhere if I stayed at home. Our economy was limited, and opportunities were few. Most of the young ladies of our island married and had children. That was our life. I had to get away if I was to fulfill my dreams.

In 1970, I immigrated to the United States to study in New York, and there I became a legal secretary. Not long after I graduated, I met a wonderful man, and we were married in December of 1974. Two years later, we started our family, and God blessed us with three wonderful sons. My plans to become a missionary were temporarily put on hold.

I discovered that rearing children in my adopted country was totally different from rearing children in our Latin countries. I was trusting God to give me His grace, so that we could bring up our boys in a loving, God-fearing environment. We taught them to love all mankind, regardless of the color of their skin, and to respect themselves and others. With God's help we began to teach them right from wrong, instilling the Golden Rule into them. God has rewarded us, and today we have three exceptional young men.

The Lord was good to us, and in the summer of 1979 we were able to buy our first home. It was in Queens Village, New York. The older boys, then three and two, were excited to have a yard to play in and to have a room each for themselves. I got busy cleaning the house and planting flowers in the yard.

We found a nice Spirit-filled church in the area where we could worship, and then it was time to get acquainted with our neighbors. I went from house to house introducing myself and the children and letting everyone know that we were the new neighbors on the block. I was surprised to find that one of our closest neighbors did not seem very happy to meet us. I was sure that would change. We were neighbors, after all.

We greeted her whenever we saw her in her yard or in the street, but she wasn't warming to us. Then one day the boys were playing ball in the yard, and their ball flew over the fence into her yard. Without thinking, one of the boys went over into her yard to retrieve the ball.

Suddenly I heard someone shouting. "Get out of my yard," she was saying, "and don't come back." I looked out to see what was happening and saw one of the boys come running out of her yard. He had left the ball behind.

I called the boys into the house and explained to them that they would have to try harder not to let the ball go over into the neighbor's yard. They tried, but when several incidents took place over the next few years, the neighbor eventually asked that the boys not even "touch" her fence. And she stopped speaking to us altogether.

One day we were in the house having lunch with some visitors, when we all smelled smoke. We got up and looked around the house, but we couldn't see anything wrong. We decided to look outside. As soon as we opened the door, we saw smoke coming from the neighbor's windows and doors.

I knew she was in the house because she had recently came home from the hospital with a new baby girl. We wondered how either of them could survive with so much smoke in the house.

"Run and call the fire department," my husband said to me. "I'm going to go in there and try to get them out." He ran for the neighbor's yard, and I ran to call 911.

The neighbor's house was locked, and my husband had to break in. He found the woman and her baby and brought them out. Then he went back in to see if he could put out the fire, which had started in the basement.

By this time, many of our neighbors had gathered to see what was happening. The fire truck arrived and finished putting out the fire.

Our neighbor did not thank us for what we had done. She still could not bring herself to speak to us. She had gone to the house of another neighbor and was looking out safely from there at what was happening. The next day, her husband did make a point of thanking us for saving the life of his wife and baby.

I kept praying and believing for God to change that woman. I wanted to see her become a kind and caring neighbor. I prayed, "God, if there is something we can do or if there is something we should not, something that is causing her to be this way with us, please show me and help us to do whatever is necessary." I knew that nothing was impossible with God, and I was trusting Him for this very practical need we had.

When things looked dim, I refused to get discouraged or doubt God. The answer seemed to be taking a long time to come, but we were not about to give up.

We had the promise of God's Word:

> [He] is able to do exceeding abundantly above all that we ask or think, according to the power that worketh in us.   Ephesians 3:20

God always goes beyond our expectations, and that's what happened in this case. I had asked Him to make my neighbor a kinder person, but He answered by making this woman my friend and a sister in the Lord. She was saved and baptized with the Holy Ghost.

I hadn't heard about this, and one day my neighbor met me on the sidewalk and spoke to me. She not only spoke to me; she asked if she could come to my house. She had some things she wanted to talk over. I was very surprised, to say the least, and was wondering what had brought about this dramatic change.

I told her I would be very happy for her to come over. She came the following evening, and it was then that she told me the good news of her being born again. She apologized for all of the wrong things she had said and done to our family. She even thanked us for the time we saved her life and the life of her baby.

She then told me why she had hated us. It was, she said, a spirit of jealousy. I wasn't sure why she should

Chapter Three

My First Missionary Endeavors

The church we had begun attending, Bethlehem Missionary Church of Queens, was just the kind of church I had always longed to be involved with. Pastor Stanley Kidd and his people had a wonderful missionary program. Every year they sent teams into different countries to work for the Lord. Eventually, I would become involved in these missionary activities.

First, though, I began to visit nursing homes and hospitals right there at home. I helped to feed sick and homeless people, and I also ministered to them spiritually. We did lots of street evangelism, too, with tract distribution and personal witnessing. I had to learn to be a soul-winner.

have been jealous of us, but I accepted her apology. That woman is still serving God today and is still one of my best friends.

I urge you today: if someone has been unkind to you, has done you wrong, has spoken ill of you, has lied about you, stolen from you or otherwise caused you pain, ask God to change that person and make that one your best friend. If you are the problem, ask Him to change you. When we ask Jesus to make us better people, He does.

He forgives us for all our wrongs and He helps us to do better. He promised:

> *Him that cometh to me I will in no wise cast out.*   John 6:37

He will never turn you away. He will help you.

I was learning to reach out to those around me, and it was time, for God had some greater things in mind for us.

My first experience with street evangelism was memorable. A couple came walking along together. I approached them and asked if they would allow me to give them a tract to read. They brushed me off and told me to get away from them. I was so embarrassed and hurt at the way they had spoken to me that I put the tracts in my pocketbook and went immediately to get a bus back home. I cried all the way home and told the Lord that I wouldn't be giving out tracts anymore. People were too cruel.

For the next few weeks, I didn't go out in street evangelism, but I wasn't very happy about it. I kept praying about what I should do.

One afternoon, as I was praying, I heard a voice. It said, "Don't be afraid or hurt when someone refuses you or pushes you away. It is not you they are refusing or pushing away. It is Me they are refusing."

I immediately got up from my knees, took some tracts, and went back out on the street to testify. Since that first rejection, I have grown a lot spiritually, and I can accept anything people do or say to me. I realize that it is not me they are refusing, but God. And, over the years, I have developed a very deep love for tract ministry. These tiny evangelists are powerful witnesses for the Lord.

My first overseas mission trip was to Jamaica, West Indies, in 1987. Eighteen of us went from the church on that trip. It was such a wonderful and rewarding trip that I again became convinced that this was what God wanted me to do. And I wanted to do it just as much as He wanted me to.

On the way to Jamaica, my brother-in-law and I were discussing the money exchange. We multiplied the money I had taken to spend by the current rate of exchange and discovered that I would have five thousand Jamaican dollars. I felt very rich. I had never spent that much money myself before. Surely I could do anything I wanted in Jamaica.

The mission trip was a life-changing experience for me. I had never experienced such a thrilling presence of the Holy Ghost being manifested. God worked through us to minister to the needs of the people.

The first person the Spirit led me to was an elderly man in a wide-brimmed hat. He was carrying a bottle of some sort of tonic. I approached him and offered him a tract. As we were speaking, the Lord told me to give him $100 Jamaican money. I thought that was strange, but I was obedient to the Lord and gave him the money.

The man hugged me and started crying. He said he knew that God had sent me to him, and he told me his story. He had left home early that morning with the bottle he had in his hand and had walked into town. He was to deliver the bottle to a man who had promised to pay him for it, and he desperately needed the money to buy food. He had not eaten for two days and had no money for bus fare.

When he got to the house where he was to deliver the bottle of tonic, the people weren't home. He waited for hours, but no one returned. Finally, he did not know what to do and began wandering around town praying. Because the sale of his tonic had not gone through, he was asking the Lord to please let someone give him something to eat, even if it was no more than a piece of bread, so that he could get enough strength to walk back home. With what I was led to give him, he was able to buy food and to take the bus back home.

I was so thankful to God that I had been obedient to Him. In the coming days, this miracle was repeated over and over again, as the Lord led me to give away the entire $5,000. In the end, I had to borrow money to buy some small souvenirs for my children.

In another incident in downtown Kingston, there was a park area where many people were shopping and just "hanging out." I stood for a while looking at the people and seeking guidance about whom I should give tracts to. I didn't want to give them to just anyone, but to those who were genuinely hungry for the Lord.

The Lord led me to an old man sitting on a bench. He appeared to be nearly ninety years old, and he had a cane in his hand.

"Hello," I said, "I'm a missionary from New York. I'm here to tell you that God loves you. I would like to give you a tract to read."

The man startled me by shouting out in tongues in the Spirit for several minutes. I waited until he had finished.

Then he said to me in English, "I know you are a messenger from God. I have been praying to God and reading the Bible, especially the Psalms, every day, twice a day. I have been asking God to show me that He was really real and was coming back to Earth to take His people. If it was true, I asked the Lord to give me a sign: "Let someone come to me while I am sitting in the park and tell me that You love me."

He had been coming to the park every day for the past two years.

After telling me this, the man raised his hands toward Heaven and said to God, "Now, Father, take me home. Let me come to You."

I was deeply touched by the faith of this old man who had waited so patiently for God to answer his prayer. His doubts were vanquished, and he knew now that God was real. I was so glad that I had been obedient and given that man a tract.

I quickly learned that whatever God tells us to do, even if it makes no sense to others, He has something wonderful in mind. He delights in working through us to bless others. What an awesome God we serve!

Many years had passed since God had placed a simple desire in my heart to become a missionary. Now, I was realizing that dream. How thrilled I was!

The next year, I accompanied a large group from the church to Belize in Central America, and again, the Lord used us in a mighty way. Many souls came to know Christ.

The work in Belize was so fruitful and the needs of the people there were so great that Pastor Kidd decided to make another trip the following year. The people of Belize needed the Word of God, they needed encouragement, and they needed uplifting. But they needed much more. They needed food, clothing, Bibles and other types of Christian materials, and we would spend the coming months gathering those things and preparing to take them to Belize. We were very excited about what the Lord would do there.

Chapter Four

Chaos in Belize City

Twenty-two members of our church flew to Belize City on May 1 of 1989, and I followed them two days later. When I got there, the group was leaving the hotel to go out to do door-to-door and street witnessing. I hurriedly got ready and went with them. Many souls came to know the Lord Jesus that day. Then we went back to the hotel to prepare for afternoon and evening meetings.

The afternoon service went well. News of our being in the city was beginning to spread, we were told, and the crowd was increasing.

Later that night, we arrived at the park where the night services were to be held. It was a very clear, cool, peaceful night. The temperature was in the low to mid eighties. Many people were already gathered. The stage was set, and the chairs were nearly full. We were anticipating a wonderful service.

Soon, the service got under way, with the wife of the assistant pastor of the church in Belize City leading the song service. For some reason, I felt a spirit of heaviness in the place. It was obvious that something was wrong. The song service was not going well at all.

Pastor Kidd noticed it too. He asked several of our people to get up and help with the singing. We prayed for them. Before long, that spirit of heaviness was broken and the worship began to flow.

As we were singing and praising God, the assistant pastor there in Belize City suddenly took the microphone and started speaking in tongues. It seemed as if he could not stop. He then spoke in English and said, "Devil, I see you. I see you, devil. You have come to steal, kill and destroy these people, but I bind you in the name of Jesus. I come against you in the name of Jesus. I command you to leave this place in the name of Jesus. I cover these people with the blood of Jesus."

He went back to speaking in tongues for a little while and then returned to English again. He did this several times and then gave the microphone back to the praise leaders.

We began to sing a chorus that everyone knew:

There is power, power, wonder-working power,
In the blood of the Lamb.
There is power, power, wonder-working power
In the precious blood of the Lamb.

And we could feel the power in that name. Then we started singing another chorus:

I command you, Satan, in the name of the Lord,
To put down your weapons and flee,
For the Lord has given me authority
To tramp all over thee.

While we were singing that, a man suddenly came running into the service dressed like a ninja in a black shirt, black pants and black shoes, and he had a black cloth of some sort over his head. He was tall and thin, and he held two machetes, one in each hand. (Some call these long knives *cutlasses*. Most machetes are about three feet long, and many are shaped like a "c" at the tip.) Without warning, the man began to chop people left and right with his two machetes.

I hadn't seen him yet myself. I heard screams and saw people running and falling, and I started to run too. Although I wasn't sure why everyone was running, I knew it had to be something serious.

I tripped over a fallen chair and fell hard to the ground. As I was falling, I felt something hit me hard on the head. I got up as quickly as I could, but as I did, I felt an even harder blow to my back.

I was knocked back to the ground. This time, instead of trying to stand, I crawled on my hands and knees over and around the chairs to escape.

When I was able to get back up, my head felt very odd, as if something was hanging from it. Then I felt something warm flowing down my neck and back. I reached up to see what it was, and my hand came away covered with blood.

I threw off the blood onto the ground and searched to see where it was coming from. I felt no pain in my head at the moment, only in my back, but there was a huge gash in my head.

I was pushing the flesh back into place to try to stop the bleeding, when I heard a voice behind me. It said, "You are going to die."

I looked back, but there was no one there. Immediately, I raised both of my hands toward Heaven and shouted aloud, "Father, You did not bring me to Belize to die. If it is my time to die, please take care of my children and my husband. But if it is Your will that I live, help me now."

By this time, I was soaked with blood. It was not only running down my neck and back; it was going down my legs and into my shoes. I looked around to see where our people were, and for the first time I saw the man. He was dressed all in black, and only his eyes were visible. He was still chopping at people on the platform.

Someone jumped off the platform, trying to flee, and others were in a state of sheer panic. There was running from one end of the large platform to the other.

Finally, the assistant pastor was able to hit the attacker with the heavy base of the microphone. When it struck his chest, it caused the black cloth that had been covering his face to fall off, and when this happened, he turned and ran. As he did, the people who were left began to throw whatever they could get in their hands at him.

I ran toward the van that had brought us to the meeting, and I could see that other injured people were there already. "My head is cut!" someone screamed. "My hand is cut!" another shouted. I heard others saying, "My fingers are cut!" "My back! My back!" and there were cries of "Oh God! Oh God!"

Screams rose from every direction, and people continued to run and jump over chairs in an attempt to escape harm. As the man with the machetes ran off, the area was left in chaos.

The pastors quickly began trying to gather the injured into the van. When they had everyone, they immediately headed off for the hospital.

The chaos that had rained down upon us in that otherwise tranquil place had seemed to go on forever, but in reality, I was told, it had lasted only a minute or two. In that short time, the man had wounded ten of us, and some of our injuries were serious.

On the way to the hospital, prayers were being sent up to God on our behalf. The people in the van took off their shirts and slips to help stop the bleeding in those of us who were the most seriously injured.

Each time my heart beat, blood gushed from my head wound. I seemed to see hundreds of tiny lights in front of me. I was asking God not to let me lose consciousness. Someone sat next to me and held my neck tight, while I held the head wound closed so that I would not lose so much blood.

The pastor of the church in Belize was driving the van, and he went as fast as he possibly could. He kept blowing his horn at cars in his way and doing whatever he could to get us to the hospital quickly. Still, it took us about forty minutes to reach the place, for it was quite far.

We arrived at the hospital to find that most of the doctors had already gone home for the day. They had to be called back in to attend to us. Doctors from other area hospitals were also called.

The emergency room was small, and most of us were kept in the hallway. I was judged to be the most severely injured patient, so they started working on me first. By this time, it was not obvious what color my clothing had been. Everything was blood-soaked.

I had not yet paid much attention to the wound on my back. It was hurting more than my head, but the head wound concerned me more at the moment. As time went on, I began to feel like my back was split wide open.

Doctors got busy on the wife of the assistant pastor (who had a cut over her left eye) and on a brother who had come with us from New York (who had four fingers severely slashed). His little finger was hanging. As other doctors arrived, they attended to the less severely wounded.

Because I was so covered with blood, the doctors could not immediately tell where I was injured. I kept telling them it was my head and my back. They cut off my clothes and all my hair so that they could get to the wounds. I heard a nurse asking the doctor not to take off all my hair. His response was, "We cannot worry about that right now."

The scissors were so dull they made a screeching noise. The doctor kept yelling, "Bring me some sharp scissors."

All this time, I was holding the large flap of skin on my head down to keep the bleeding to a minimum. Once they had removed my hair, the doctors began to clean the wound and work to stop the bleeding and keep me from losing consciousness.

The news of this attack traveled fast, and Christians, on their way home from other churches in the city, heard the news on the radio. They went straight to the hospital and stayed there praying until all of us were out of danger. They prayed so intensely, in fact, that doctors were forced to ask them to move outside. They stood by the entrance to the emergency room crying out to God for miracles for us.

We needed them.

Chapter Five

Miracle Upon Miracle

As it became more and more difficult for me to remain conscious, the doctors kept slapping me on the side of my face and asking me what my name was and where I lived. Finally, I asked them, "Why are you asking me the same questions over and over. I've already told you many times."

"We just want to be sure you are still with us," one of them answered.

After stitching up my head, they took me for x-rays. Four x-rays were taken. A little later, one of the doctors appeared, holding the x-rays in his hand and saying, "You have a fractured skull. We must do surgery on your head. I will have to call in a surgeon because there is none on duty right now. He should be here between four-thirty and five-thirty."

I lay on that emergency room bed for the next several hours, crying out loud to God. I said, "God, You did not bring me to Belize to have surgery, but to do Your work. Please, God, fix my head. Fix the x-rays so that when the surgeon comes he will not be able to find anything. I need a miracle, and I know that You can do it. Thank You for fixing my head." I was praying in tongues and in English, believing God with all my heart for the miracle to be done.

Several hours later, I was still in the emergency room lying in that bed, when suddenly I felt as though cold water were pouring from my body. A nurse was attending to a nearby patient, and I called to her, "Nurse, I'm cold." I also noticed that I was perspiring profusely.

The nurse took one look at me and started running. Within seconds, she returned with two doctors. They hooked up an extra intravenous apparatus to my other arm, and opened them both up fully. They hung two more bags of some solution and turned them on. Slowly, I warmed up and stopped perspiring so terribly.

I asked the doctor what had happened, and he told me that my body had been completely depleted of salts. If they had not been able to restore my liquids, I would have lapsed into a coma and could have died.

My condition improved, and they were able to clean me up more and to take me to a room upstairs. Pastor Kidd left two sisters to stay at my bedside to keep me awake and attend to my needs. A nurse was also assigned to me.

Finally, around five-thirty that next morning, the doctor and the surgeon he had called came into my room together. The surgeon had the x-rays in his hand. He said, "Good morning, Mrs. Narain. I am Dr. Jacobs, the surgeon who will be doing the surgery on your head." He placed the x-rays up on the frame so he could read them, and I saw a strange expression come over his face. I could not tell whether he was thinking it was either good or bad, but he looked amazed.

He turned to the doctor and asked, "Are you sure we have the right x-rays?"

"Yes," the doctor replied, but to be sure, he checked the name on the x-rays.

"Mrs. Narain, right?" he asked. I nodded.

The surgeon looked at the x-rays again for a while. Then he said to me, "Well, Mrs. Narain, I have good news for you. I do not see a fracture on this x-ray, so I will not have to do surgery."

I shouted, "I've been touched! Hallelujah! Thank You, Jesus!"

The two doctors stepped outside of the room, but I could still hear what one of them was saying. "I don't understand this. I know I saw a fracture." The doctor knew that when he first saw the x-rays, they showed an apparent fracture. Now there was none.

All this time, our members who had not been injured were there praying and crying out to God on our behalf. And God was answering those prayers.

I hadn't realized it yet, but the Lord had warned me two weeks before of what was to come. One night, two weeks before the trip, I had been awakened by a frightening dream. I dreamed that I was in some sort of church service in a strange country. I saw many chairs, and suddenly people were running and screaming, and there was lots of blood. I woke up screaming and frightened.

My screaming woke up my husband. He held me in his arms and asked me if I was okay. I told him about the dream. "Well," he asked, "was any of the blood on you?"

For some reason, I could not remember. I later came to the conclusion that if I had remembered the dream more clearly, and if the blood had been on me, I probably would not have gone to Belize. Over the years, most of my dreams had come true. Some of my friends and family members had even come to call me "the dreamer." God wanted me in Belize City. He was just getting me ready for what would happen there.

Then, just a week before the trip, I dreamed I was

in a hospital, going from room to room, witnessing and praying for sick people. I went into one room, and there was a woman in the bed who had three children. I recognized the woman and asked her, "What are you doing in here? You don't belong here. I'm going to speak with the doctor and see if I can get you out of here." Then I continued on to other rooms, fully intending to find her doctor and speak with him about her release.

As I made my rounds of the hospital rooms in the dream, I noticed that they were all separated by peach-colored curtains, and each room had white walls. Before I could get to the doctor to have the woman released from the hospital, I woke up.

The morning after the incident in Belize, when it started to become daylight in the room, I was still awake (because the doctors were afraid to let me go to sleep). I suddenly noticed that the curtains around me were peach-colored, just as those in my dream. I turned to one of the sisters who were sitting near me and said to her, "Hurry! Hurry! Look outside and tell me what color the rest of the curtains are."

She looked out and said, "They're peach, just like these."

Then I asked, "See what color the walls are."

She replied, "They're white!"

When she said that, I knew the meaning of my dream. I cried out, "Oh, my God!"

The sister asked me what was wrong and why I had wanted to know the color of the curtains and the walls. Then I told her about the dream God had given to me.

That morning, when Pastor Kidd came to see me, he first asked how I was feeling, and then he told me he was going to speak with the doctor and ask him how soon I would be able to travel back to the U.S. He was concerned about the quality of the hospital. The staff and supplies were very limited. Even the sheets could not be changed on a daily basis. "You don't belong in here," Pastor Kidd said. He felt responsible to get me back to America to some better medical facility.

I and the sister with me were astonished at his words. They were the exact same words I had spoken to the lady in my dream. I had dreamed them a week before, and now my pastor was saying them to me. I came to the conclusion that I was the lady in the dream. Like me, she had three children.

God was working. He had done many great miracles for me already the night before. For instance, the doctor had told me I needed a blood transfusion because of all the blood I had lost. My blood count was way below normal. When he told me this, I cried out to God again and asked Him to please bring my blood count back up to what it should be. If I didn't get at least two pints of blood, the doctor insisted, I would pass out when I tried to sit up or walk.

After I had an assurance that God would do a miracle, I declined to accept the blood transfusion. I told the doctor that I was believing God to give me the blood I needed and to bring my blood count back to what it should be.

My pastor came and spoke with me the next morning. He said he would have someone from the group give the blood I needed. I told him that I was believing God for another miracle. He had already done so many that I knew He could do one more, and that He would. If I absolutely had to have a blood transfusion, I said, my husband would come and give it.

When the doctor kept insisting that if I didn't have the blood I would faint when I bent over, I made a bargain with him. "If I pass out, give me the blood," I told him. "But if I don't pass out, I don't want it."

He said, "I don't want to take that chance. It could be dangerous. You could lapse into a coma and never come out of it." I assured him that God would do the work and keep me safe.

In the end, I didn't have to take the blood transfusion, and I never passed out, even when I bent over, sat up or walked. I give all the glory to God. He answered my prayer and took care of me.

My pastor asked the doctor to let him know just as soon as he thought I was well enough to travel back to the U.S. On the fourth day, he considered that my recovery was progressing sufficiently that I could go home. They had been sitting me up and moving me around, and I was doing fine.

All of those from our group who were injured came back home to New York on the fifth day after the attack. It was disappointing to miss the rest of the missionary activities in Belize, but I had been able to witness to my principal doctor, to two nurses and to three patients in nearby rooms, and all of them accepted the Lord as their personal Savior. It was just as I had seen in my dream.

Just the fact that I was alive was a miracle. The way God worked through the doctors with their limited resources was a miracle. I experienced God's healing power, and I learned that when you truly trust God with all your heart, He never fails you. He always comes through. I had trusted God with all I had, and He answered me and granted me everything I asked Him for.

Glory be to His name! Through it all, He had been honored.

Chapter Six

God's Protection

As I arrived back in America, I became very much aware of how blessed I was and of how God had protected me from something much more serious. Several weeks before we had left for Belize, the church had been in revival meetings. One night, when the preacher called everyone to come up front for prayer, I found myself standing at the back of the crowd in the middle aisle.

I was in deep praise, with both hands raised toward Heaven, when suddenly I felt a hand touch me. It began at the top of my head on the left side and moved all the way down to my lower back. A chill ran through my body, and I looked around to see who was behind me praying for me. I was surprised to see that no one was there.

All of the people were still in front of me, and they were in deep praise too, unaware of what was happening with me. The spot where that hand touched me was the exact place where my head was later cut. I came to believe that God had anointed that spot because of what was to take place.

Before I left for Belize, I had told several people what had happened to me. They, too, were convinced that the Lord was anointing me for something special, although no one could have guessed what it might be.

The hand I felt moving down my back felt very much like the blood that later flowed down it and into my shoes. I am convinced that if God had not anointed that spot on my head, I would not be here today to write about this experience.

My family and our church family received me with open arms, and we rejoiced together over my deliverance.

My children had suffered more than anyone else over the incident. The boys were eight, eleven and twelve at the time of the attack, and they were understandably horrified by it. The two older ones understood it more and could not comprehend why God would allow something so terrible to happen to their mom while she was working for Him. They felt that God should have taken better care of me.

The oldest child, Edwin, became angry with God. He stopped praying and did not want to go to church. At school, he was noticeably quiet and standoffish. His teachers could not help but notice, and one of them called Edwin over and asked him what was wrong. At first, Edwin didn't want to talk about it, but the teacher convinced him he would feel better if he did.

Finally, Edwin told his teacher about the attack I had suffered and how he was angry at God for letting it happen. The teacher, fortunately, was wise enough to answer well. He explained to Edwin that God sometimes permits things to happen for reasons we can't understand at the time. God knows the reason, and someday it might also become apparent to us. He also assured Edwin that I would be fine and encouraged him to tell God that he was sorry for being angry with Him. Later that night, before he went to bed, Edwin knelt and prayed and asked God for forgiveness.

Our middle son, Marty, told me how they had learned of the attack. Their dad had called them all to the bedroom, and there he sat down with them and told them what had happened to me.

"Dad," Marty responded, "don't kid. That's not funny."

God's Protection **45**

His dad assured him that he was not kidding. It was true. Then he assured them that he was certain I would be all right. God was in control, I had left under His protection, and He would bring me back home safely.

When Marty first saw me after I got back (with all my hair cut off), he was horrified. He knew the story about Samson's hair being his strength, and he thought it must be the same for me. In his eyes, I suddenly looked very weak.

If anything, our youngest son, Garin, was even more concerned than the others about my being okay. Being the smallest of the three, he was very anxious to see me again.

All the children were glad that I was alive, and they were waiting for the day I could come home. Their father wisely took time to explain the situation to them in detail and to answer any questions they had.

After I got back home, I assured the boys that God knew exactly what He was doing when He allowed this terrible thing to happen. He was in control of everything. My sons wondered what would happen to the man who had done this thing to their mother.

He had hidden from the authorities for several days, but on the third day after the incident he was caught with both machetes still in his possession, and he was placed in jail. When the judge asked him if he had done this thing and why, he admitted that he had and said it was because he did not like the hymns we were singing. He had watched us for some twenty minutes from the shadows before striking.

The five people from Belize who were injured were not willing to press charges against the man, fearing that he would come after them when he was released. Because of this, officials could no longer hold him after he had served a total of eight months for his crime. So, he was set free.

Rumor had it that the man was mentally disturbed, and before leaving the country, I had voiced my request that if the man was really mentally ill, he should not be imprisoned. He needed help. In his sick mind, he had intended to do us serious harm, but God had protected us.

Chapter Seven

Complete Restoration

My recuperation was not a foregone conclusion, at least as far as the doctor who attended me in Belize City was concerned. Before I left the hospital, he warned me that the cut on my head would affect me for the rest of my life. I should never expect to be the same again.

I was sure that he was wrong. We were trusting God to heal me completely, and He did. He also granted me a continuance of sound mind.

There were scars from the attack. I have a "c" marked in my head and a straight slash scar on my back, and those will no doubt be with me until the day I die. The man cut me on the head with the machete with the "c" shape on the tip, and he cut me on the back with the straight machete. But those scars only serve as a daily reminder of God's healing power.

The God we serve has promised us great things. The apostle Paul wrote:

> *Now unto him that is able to do exceeding abundantly above all that we ask or think, according to the power that worketh in us, unto him be glory in the church by Christ Jesus throughout all ages, world without end. Amen.*
>
> Ephesians 3:20-21

I have absolutely no aftereffect from the cuts I suffered, and I do not intend to have any in the future. The God we serve is a God of completion. If He had started a work in my physical body, He would complete it.

I came away from Belize knowing that God had spared my life because He was not finished with me yet. He had more for me to do, and I was determined to do it. If He had been finished with me here, He would have taken me home. But He spared my life because He had much more for me to do.

Since the time of the attack in Belize City, I have been able to go on many more mission trips to other countries. God has used me to preach His Word, to help the sick and suffering, and to counsel with those in need. He has also given me a wonderful tract ministry.

When this tract ministry began, the Lord told me He would enable my tracts to go throughout the world, even to countries I would not be able to go to personally. He inspired me to write the tracts, and He showed me ways to distribute them to those who have need of them. (For those who are interested, you can find a list of available tracts and an address for ordering them at the back of the book.) God has also given me poems and skits.

I find great joy in serving and blessing others. While I was still in the hospital in Belize, a lady and her nineteen-year-old daughter came to visit me. I couldn't help but notice that the lady had on slippers, and the girl was barefooted. While we were talking, the mother told me that she had no husband and that they were believing God for a job so that she could buy a pair of shoes for her daughter (who wanted them so that she could go to church). I was led to tell them that if they would come to the hotel where I was staying after I was released I would give them some shoes. They came, and I gave them two pairs of shoes and some clothes. It was a heart-rending sight to see that mother thanking God for a pair of shoes. How blessed we are! And what a joy it is to bless others!

The people of many other nations pray daily for

things that we in America take for granted. I was thrilled to be able to continue blessing people in many places, as the Lord enabled me to do it. I should have been dead or maimed, but I had completely recovered for His glory.

Chapter Eight

God Was Glorified

This whole bizarre incident does leave many questions in our minds. It is normal that small children would not understand such things, for we adults can barely understand them ourselves.

The most common question I am asked about all of this is WHY? Why would God allow this to happen? I'm not sure that I have all the answers to this question, but what is easy to see is that God was glorified through it all. Because of this incident and the publicity it generated, many hundreds of people attended the crusades there who might not have otherwise known that we were in town at all. Although the five of us from New York who were injured were sent home early, the meetings continued and many wonderful things happened. Souls were saved, marriages were restored, and lives were turned around. God was glorified.

Clearly, the devil had meant this attack for evil, for he is the thief:

> *The thief cometh not, but for to steal, and to kill, and to destroy: I am come that they might have life, and that they might have it more abundantly.* John 10:10

God, however, turned the tables on Satan, and He brought forth good out of the incident.

The second question I am often asked is would I ever go again. Not only would I, but I have gone, as I said, many times since then. I haven't had the opportunity to return to Belize, but I have a great desire to do that too (and to speak with the man who did this thing). Wouldn't it be wonderful if I could lead him to the feet of Jesus? I would even love to go back to that park where it all happened and have a few nights of evangelistic meetings.

Am I not afraid to go again? No! I'm not. God is with us, and we have nothing to fear.

Once, when I was with a group in Jamaica, four of us were stranded one night out in the countryside. We had traveled out of Kingston into the countryside to do some street witnessing. Then, for some unknown reason, the bus that took us out there left, and four of us were left behind.

It was beginning to get dark, and there were no buses in sight. We managed to walk to a large open area where, we were told, buses normally stopped. There were some young men there with taxis offering to take people into town, but their prices were exorbitant, much more than we could afford. They gradually reduced their asking price as time wore on, but it was still too high.

They told us that there were no buses after seven in the evening and that there would be no possibility of our getting back to Kingston without hiring them. We were not so sure. We moved over to one side and began to pray together that God would make a way for us to get back to town.

Some of the men followed us, laughing and mocking at us, and saying that we could pray all night until the next day, and still no buses would come along.

By now, it was after eight, and it was getting very dark. We continued to pray and believe God for a miracle. Every time we joined hands to pray, the men broke out in mocking laughter. One of them said that no god was able to bring a bus to that place at that hour of the night.

Then suddenly we saw two bright lights coming toward us. It was a bus. We rushed back to the spot where the buses loaded. The driver of the bus screeched to a halt and shouted that he was in a great rush. He had gotten lost, he said, and he needed for everyone to quickly get on. "I have no time to waste!" he shouted. "I am in a rush!"

We were praising God for the miracle, and we started to get on the bus. But then I stopped. I could not leave there without speaking with those young men. I ran quickly over to where they were gathered and said to them, "You see. Our God never fails. He is still doing miracles today."

"This really is a miracle," one of the men answered. "I have never seen a bus up here this late at night."

The fact that the bus driver got lost was God's way of providing for us, and what's more, he did not charge us anything to take us back into town. He was going there anyhow, he said, so we could just ride along. Praise God!

Another good thing that came out of all this was, for me, seeing the great outpouring of love from the people of Belize. Nothing like this had ever happened in their city before, and their response was overwhelming. I was deeply touched by the kindness they showed me.

Many of the local believers came to the hospital and prayed. They were from many parts of the country. Some came by car or bus, but others came on foot, walking miles from neighboring towns, and others came on bicycles. Visitors came all day and into the night. So many came that eventually hospital authorities were forced to place security guards at my door so that I could rest.

I was very moved by the couple who were led to stop at a restaurant and buy me a special meal. They didn't know it, but that particular day I had been asking God for something special to eat.

I am deeply indebted to the nurse who left running and came back with two doctors when my body was going into shock, and to the two doctors who came running back with her. All of these experiences mold and shape our lives, and I am grateful to God for them.

Most of all, I am thankful that He was glorified through my life.

Chapter Nine

A Very Important Dream

I have told you about a dream I had before traveling to Belize for missionary work and how that dream came true. Now, here is a dream that I really want you to take to heart for your own life.

I dreamed that I saw the door of Heaven opened. Jesus stepped out of Heaven and stood there in mid-air next to the door. All of the people of the Earth were looking up toward Heaven, listening to what Jesus was saying. He was speaking to this world, and His voice was like thunder filling the whole Earth.

His appearance was so bright that I could not see His face. He was saying:

> *Many of you will not be saved because you refuse to confess Me as Lord. Many of you are even in churches, but still you have not confessed Me as I have told you to do. You must confess Me with your mouth in order to be saved. Do it quickly, for I am coming soon.*

Then the Lord stepped back into Heaven.

In my dream, many of the people on Earth began to fall to their knees in prayer, confessing God. Others went running to find someone who could help them. They wanted to confess Jesus, but they didn't know how. They could not seem to find anyone to help them.

Please, if you are reading this book and you have never confessed Jesus and asked Him to save you, do it now. If you are already saved and have confessed Him, continue to confess Him as Lord of your life. Keep living for Him so that you will be ready when He comes to take us with Him. He said that He has gone to prepare a place for you:

> *In my Father's house are many mansions: if it were not so, I would have told you. I go to prepare a place for you. And if I go and prepare a place for you, I will come again, and receive you unto myself; that where I am, there ye may be also.* John 14:2-3

One day, every knee will bow to Jesus:

> *That at the name of Jesus every knee should bow, of things in heaven, and things in earth, and things under the earth; and that every tongue should confess that Jesus Christ is Lord, to the glory of God the Father.*
>
> Philippians 2:10-11

Why not do it right now?

As I look around me today, I see far too many men and women going about their business, rushing here and there, finding excuses for not having time for God. "I am too busy," they tell me. "I have too many problems right now. What I need He is not going to do for me. Life is too hard. I need money. Money is the only thing that could help me right now."

Where does God fit into our busy lives? While He is running after us, we seem to be too busy for Him. He is patiently waiting for us to come to Him for help. You may be one of those people who can't seem to find time for God.

Are you too busy to realize that He woke you up this morning? What if He had not awakened you? What if your heart had stopped beating during the night? Or what if Jesus were to come today? Would you be ready?

Ready or not, your heart will stop beating one day.

Ready or not, Jesus is coming. If you are ready, you will go with Him. If you are not ready, you still have to go, but it won't be to Heaven with Jesus. Instead, you will go to Hell with the devil and his angels and with all those who have rejected Christ and were not willing to make Him Lord.

Can you ask death to wait a little longer because you are not ready to die? Or can you ask death to come back later so that you can make your heart right with God? No! When death comes, it will be too late. You have no choice. You have to go — ready or not. No medical technology can keep you from dying in that moment. Nothing you do can prevent death. The Scriptures declare:

> *It is appointed unto men once to die, but after this the judgment.*   Hebrews 9:27

I encourage you to take time out of your busy schedule for God. Your stay in this world is temporary. You are only passing through. You will leave this busy place one day to go to your final destination — Heaven or Hell. Now is the only time you have to prepare for that day of eternal destiny.

You cannot go to both places; it will be one or the other. If you choose to accept Jesus into your heart and live for Him until He comes back to Earth, Heaven will be your home. If you continue to neglect salvation by being too busy to think about the welfare of your soul, then Hell awaits you, and your abode will be with the devil and his angels. Hell will be filled with those who were just too busy to find time for God.

God is still awaiting your answer. He is ready to save you and to set you free from sin, but time is running out. All of the signs are pointing to the soon return of Jesus. Hurricanes, mud slides, floods, earthquakes, tornadoes, killings, wars and rumors of wars, the spread of homosexuality, children rising against parents and parents turning against children ... all of these are biblical signs pointing to the Lord's soon return. Please, don't let Him come and find you not ready.

Today, as you read this book, you can be saved. You can accept Christ into your heart and start living for Him. Paul wrote to the Roman believers:

> *That if thou shalt confess with thy mouth the Lord Jesus, and shalt believe in thine heart that God hath raised him from the dead, thou shalt be saved. For with the heart man believeth unto righteousness; and with the mouth confession is made unto salvation.* Romans 10:9-10

If you feel the need to accept Jesus into your heart and would like to do it now, please pray this prayer with me in sincerity of heart:

Jesus,

I come to You now. I want to be saved. Please forgive me for all of my sins. I believe with all my heart that You died to save me from my sins and that You rose again from the dead. I promise to love You, serve You and live for You until You return to Earth. Thank You, Lord, for saving me.

Amen!

If you sincerely prayed this prayer, Jesus has saved you and has written your name in the Lamb's Book of Life. He will now help you to live for Him.

Rejoice, for you are on your way to Heaven.

Chapter Ten

A World in Need of Love

This world is sorely lacking love. People talk about love, but they don't know how to show it. Real love comes only through Jesus Christ, and only those who love Him can truly love others.

Before we are saved and we read in the Bible where Jesus said, *"Love thy neighbor as thyself,"* we think, "He must be kidding. How can He expect us to love others as much as we love ourselves?" We think we could never love anyone that much.

But He is God, and He can do what is humanly impossible. When Jesus comes into your life and changes you, it becomes easy to love.

There have been people whom I didn't "hit it off well" with. They didn't seem to like me, and I certainly didn't like them. But I find myself praying for them and being kind to them. God's love causes us to be kind to those we know and those we don't know, those we "like" and those we don't like.

This word LOVE is so powerful that it encompasses all of the other commandments. It was meant to control the lives of all born-again Christians, and also of the unsaved in the entire world. If everyone would be governed by love, this world would not be in the horrible condition it is in. Crime would not exist.

I can imagine that many are saying, "It's too late for all that now." But it's not too late. It is never too late for love. There is always hope — even for this sinful world. God is love, and His love can change everything and everyone.

Love knows no color. It is not easily offended or insulted. It does not get hurt. It does not steal or kill or lie or hate.

Love is patient; love is kind; love does not envy or boast. It is not proud; it is not rude; it is not self-seeking; it is not easily angered; it keeps no record of wrongs. Love does not delight in evil, but rejoices in truth. It always protects, always trusts, always hopes, always perseveres, and it never fails.

When you love others, you don't want anything bad or painful to happen to them. You want only good things for them. This world is lacking this kind of love.

People everywhere are hurting, and they are looking for love. God can help you to be the person who helps them find it, who shows it to them.

God will help you to be governed by love and to learn to share it with all mankind. You will be amazed to see the response you will get. Love moves the hearts of the most hardened sinners.

It was because of God's love for us that He sent His only Son down to Earth to die for our sins:

> *For God so loved the world, that he gave his only begotten Son, that whosoever believeth in him should not perish, but have everlasting life.*
> John 3:16

God does not want us to suffer and die in our sins. He saw the sinful state of man and how he was living without love for his fellowman, so He sent His Son, Jesus, to show us love. If you are lacking love in your life, why not ask Jesus to fill you with true love, the kind of love God the Father showed toward each of us? If you know someone who is crying out for love, reach out to that person and show him love. You will be blessed, and you will feel the joy of showing love, of caring for others, of sharing love with someone in need.

This world is our practice field. If we cannot love each other here, how could we ever get along in eternity? We must love each other here before we are given the opportunity to do it there.

One of the purposes of this book is to challenge you, dear reader, to let God use you to bless those around you. He can work through each of us in ways we never imagined, and He is looking for those who will make themselves available to Him.

He is not necessarily looking for people of talent and ability. He will give us the abilities we need to do His work. There are many people of ability, but they have no availability, so God cannot use them.

Some feel that they have no time to be used of God. Where would we be if those who reached out to us would have taken this attitude? Reach out to others, as someone has reached out to you.

Some wonder what they could ever do for God. Well, we never know until we make ourselves available, do we? God may not necessarily need to use you for foreign missions, but He might. In the meantime, He can use you right here at home — in your home, your community, your place of business or your church. God can use you wherever you happen to be.

We are only vessels that He works through. We become His feet, His hands and His mouth in this world.

God is no respecter of persons, and He does not use us because we are either rich or poor. He gives no preference to skin color, name, title or nationality. He uses those who are less intelligent and those who are more intelligent. The disciples were unlearned men for the most part, yet the Lord called them to follow Him. He personally taught them and sent them out, and they accomplished great things for His glory. He will use you too.

If you are in right standing with God, and you make yourself available to Him, get ready to be used for the upbuilding of His Kingdom.

I have never been sorry for my decision to serve the Lord, to be one of His evangelists, and to take His Word to other nations. He has blessed me so. How could I do otherwise?

The Lord is my Source and has promised to meet all my needs:

> *But my God shall supply all your need according to his riches in glory by Christ Jesus.*
> Philippians 4:19

What, then, can prevent me from going forth to a world devoid of love to declare Him who is love?

Tract Ordering Information

1. Let Him Change You
2. Are You in the In-Crowd?
3. The Last Hour Is Coming
4. Where Will You Spend Eternity?
5. Which Signpost Are You?
6. Inside the Gate
7. He Did It All for Thee
8. Too Busy for God
9. Is Your Name Written in the Lamb's Book of Life?
10. My Children
11. Deception
12. Is Everything All Right?
13. A Way of Escape
14. The Broad and Narrow Road
15. How? Where? When?
16. Use Your Weapon!
17. On the Way To?
18. Don't Be Left Behind
19. Represent Me Fully
20. A New Home Prepared for You
21. This May Be You
22. Appointment
23. The Gift of Salvation
24. Love
25. A Righteous Life Is an Investment for the New Earth
26. White Robes
27. Gaining, Not Giving Up
28. Be Born Again
29. IF
30. Free or Paid
31. Servants to Evil Spirits

These tracts are sent out with the desire of leading souls to Christ Jesus. For your free copy (as the Lord provides) send a love offering and/or postage and handling to our ministry address:

THE LAST CRY TRACT MINISTRY
5601 SW 8th Court
Plantation, FL 33317

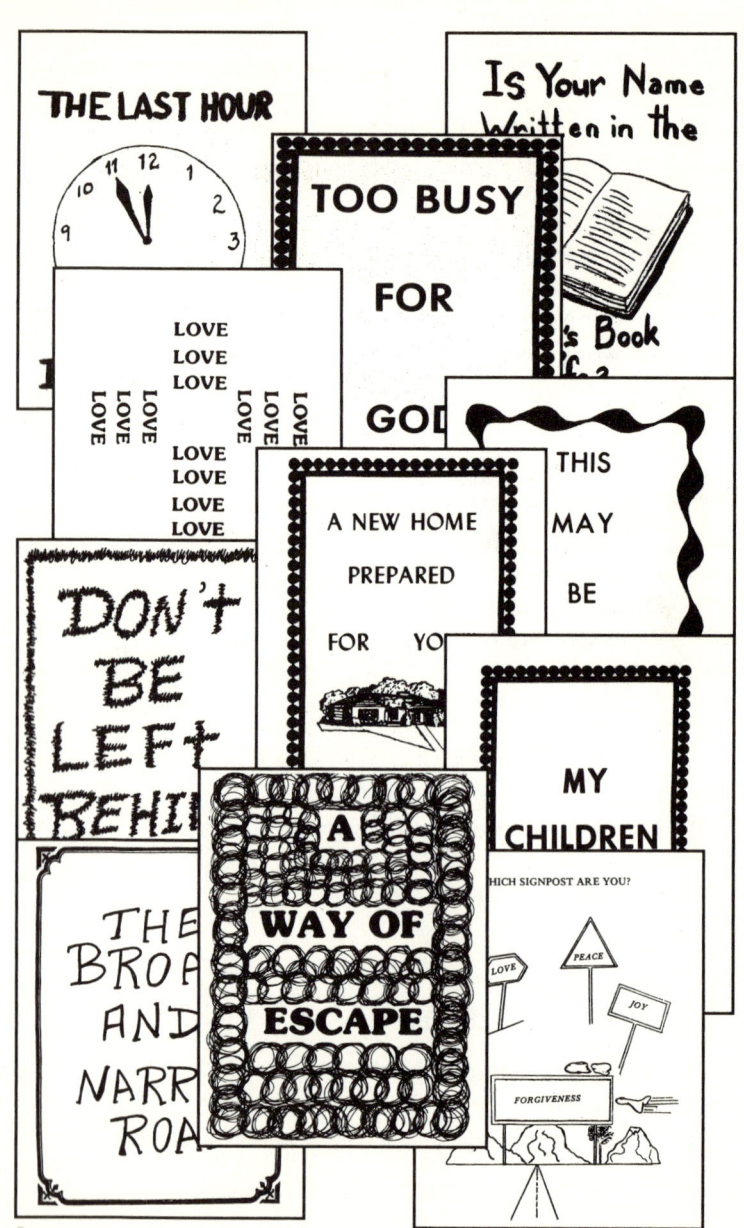

Some of the Available Tracts:
(See the following pages for ordering information.)

About the Author

Evangelist Yvonne Ruperta Narain was born in Honduras, Central America. She has been married for twenty-five years and is the mother of three sons. She grew up with a burning desire to be a missionary traveling the world and winning the lost for Christ. In 1970, she immigrated to the United States, where she pursued her dream of being a soul-winner for Jesus. Her joy is telling others about the power of Jesus and how He can change their lives.

In 1987, she had the opportunity to go on her first missionary trip, to Jamaica, West Indies. Since then, she has been evangelizing both at home and abroad.

She is a graduate of Bethlehem Missionary Bible School in Queens, New York. She is a strong believer in miracles and prayer because she knows what the power of prayer can do. She believes that you must have faith to trust God and that you should believe God for whatever you need. She knows, from experience, that with God all things are possible.

souls for Him, and I trust that reading about it has done the same for you.

I want to encourage you never to be doubtful or afraid to go out for the Lord. We serve a mighty and all-powerful God, and His promises are sure. He has promised never to leave us nor forsake us, so He will be with you at all times. He will bring you out of whatever situation you may find yourself in — if you will only remain faithful to Him and trust Him.

Epilogue

I would hate to think that my story would be an excuse for anyone being afraid to serve God in the future. It was meant to be just the opposite. Please, don't ever be afraid to go somewhere for the Lord. Go, knowing that God is with you wherever you are. When God calls you and sends you out, He always takes care of you.

Some of you might be thinking, *How can I believe that God will take care of me when something so terrible happened to this lady?* Believe me, God knows what He is doing. He could have prevented this attack from happening, but He permitted it to happen for a reason. He took care of those of us who were attacked. Our lives were spared, and no one was left disabled.

I feel satisfied to know that God has received glory from all this, and I trust that He will continue to receive glory from it. The experience has given me an even stronger desire to live for Christ and to win lost

Please don't be too busy or too much in a hurry to tell others how you feel about them. It is important to express it. If you love someone, don't take it for granted that they know. Make sure you tell them. It is good to know that others love you and care about you, and you must return the favor.

After the unexpected and unprovoked attack I suffered in Belize, I decided not only to tell people that I love them, but also to show them and make them feel loved and special. I hope you will do the same. This is the reason Jesus said that the greatest commandment was to love Him, and the second was to love one another. On that commandment, He said, hangs all other laws. Let us continue in love until Jesus comes.

In my distress I cried unto the LORD, *and he heard me.* Psalm 120:1

Don't Wait Until I'm Gone

Take time out to show each other
How much we love and care.

Each moment that comes is precious
And will not come again.
So say and do the things that you'll
Be glad you say and do.

When those moments are past and gone,
No use you mumbling on
About the things you could have done
After I'm dead and gone.

You cannot bring those moments back
You failed to use correctly.
You only have the memories and regrets
Of things you didn't do.

So, take time now and show me
How much you care for me.
Find time now to tell me
How much you cherish me.

Don't wait until I'm dead and gone
To brag and carry on
About how much you loved me
After I'm dead and gone.

period, but one stands out in my memory. One relative, when he came to visit me, hugged and kissed me. He said he had been praying for me since the moment he had learned of the incident. "I asked God to spare your life so that I could see you again," he said, "and it's because I needed to tell you something." I wondered what was so important to him that he had sought God so.

"I want you to know that I love you," he told me, "and that you're a special person to me. I knew that I loved you and thought the world of you, but I had never taken the time to tell you. Now, God gave me another opportunity."

I thanked him for his expression of love and told him that I loved him too. Then, after he had gone, I wrote a poem that I would like to dedicate here to my entire family, to my friends and to you:

Don't Wait Until I'm Gone
by Yvonne Narain

Don't wait until I'm dead and gone
To show how much you care.
Don't wait until I cannot hear
To say how much you love me.

While you and I are here,
Let's find time to share.

Chapter Twelve

Don't Wait Until I'm Gone

The day the five of us who were wounded in Belize returned to America, we were greeted by an unusual outpouring of love and sympathy at the airport. All of our immediate family members, plus all the church people were there to greet us. What an experience it was! The gratefulness and thanksgiving we held in our hearts to the Lord as we greeted each other was deeply moving.

During my recovery period, my family and the church family supported me totally. The church people brought me good food that helped to restore my strength and replenish my blood.

There were many touching moments during that

ing for you to come to Him so that He can heal you and give you the miracle you need.

The same Jesus who delivered me from the hand of a man who wanted to take my life can heal you right now. Because there is power in prayer, I am here today to tell this story. God answered my prayer and the prayers of all those who were interceding for me. I am happy to report that all ten of those who were injured in the attack in Belize City are in good health and doing well today. Thank God for His miracle-working power. Let it touch your life today.

ited Him. We have felt that He could only do so much.

No, friends, it is time to say to God, "Father, I'm taking the limits off You, and I'm believing You to do the impossible for me." Don't do this only with your sickness. Do it with every area of your life.

Never become discouraged and give up. As long as you have life, there is hope for your situation, for *"with God all things are possible."*

> *But Jesus beheld them, and said unto them, With men this is impossible; but with God all things are possible.*   *Matthew 19:26*

God has given doctors wisdom to help us and to diagnose our illnesses, but doctors don't have the final say over our lives. God does. God changes situations in people's lives when they trust Him and believe Him to do it for them. He did it for me, and He can do it for you today.

My healing and physical recovery were not automatic. I had to refuse to accept the verdict the doctor gave me, and I had to believe what God said instead. I had to trust that He could do all things.

God is still the Miracle Worker. The same Jesus who walked the Earth two thousand years ago — healing the blind, the deaf, the crippled and the lame, and even raising the dead — is still alive today. He is wait-to be for you. Believe Him to heal you and do for you what the doctors, your therapist, your mother and father, your sister or brother, your husband or wife, your friends or any other person cannot do for you. He said in His Word:

> *I am the LORD that healeth thee.*
> Exodus 15:26

> *He was wounded for our transgression, he was bruised for our iniquities: the chastisement of our peace was upon him; and with his stripes we are healed.* Isaiah 53:5

Jesus said that healing was *"the children's bread"* (Matthew 15:26). The thirty-nine stripes that He took on His back were for our healing. Any disease or illness you may have, He will heal you if you just ask Him. God has already provided the healing for us. All we have to do is accept it by confessing it with our mouths, believing it in our hearts and receiving it into our spirits. Then the healing will manifest in our bodies.

The healing God provided is already done in the spirit realm. We just need to let it manifest in the natural (our bodies) by confessing it daily. We need to take the limits off of God. For too long, we have lim-

Chapter Eleven

By His Stripes

The miracles God has done on my own body have given me even more faith to reach out and help others who are suffering physically. You might have some kind of illness, a sickness or disease, and perhaps doctors have given you a negative report. No matter how impossible your case may seem, there is hope for you in the Great Physician.

You may have come to the conclusion that there is no remedy, no solution for your problem. But I have good news for you. God is able to do the impossible, and He can do it for you.

God can do all things, great or small. He is the Problem Solver, the Healer. He is anything you need Him